01233167

SUPER
SCARY ART

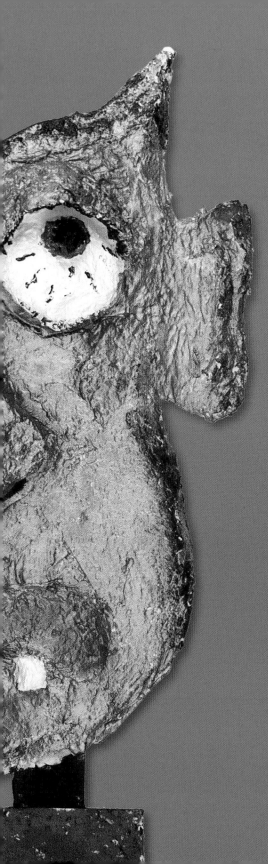

Thanks to the creative team:
Editor: Tim Harris
Design: Perfect Bound Ltd

Original edition copyright 2019 by
Hungry Tomato Ltd.
Copyright © 2019 by Lerner Publishing Group, Inc.

Hungry Tomato® is a trademark of
Lerner Publishing Group

Hungry Tomato®
A division of Lerner Publishing Group, Inc.
241 First Avenue North
Minneapolis, MN 55401 USA

For reading levels and more information, look up
this title at www.lernerbooks.com.

Main body text set in CocogooseNarrow Semi Light.

Library of Congress Cataloging-in-Publication Data

The Cataloging-in-Publication Data for *Super Scary
Art* is on file at the Library of Congress.
ISBN 978-1-5415-0130-0 (lib. bdg.)
ISBN 978-1-5415-4286-0 (eb pdf)

Manufactured in the United States of America
1-43800-33646-8/10/2018

SUPER
SCARY ART

EMILY KINGTON

HUNGRY
TOMATO™

MINNEAPOLIS

CONTENTS

SUPER SCARY ART 5
TOP TIPS 5
MATERIALS 6
TOOLS AND TECHNIQUES 7

GARGOYLE DOOR DECORATION 8

SCARY SPIDER FAMILY PAPERWEIGHT 10

UGLY FISH BANK 14

FRANKENSTEIN COAT HANGER 18

BASKET SKULL 22

MONSTER PEN PAL 26

BEASTLY BATS 28
SUPPLIES 32

SUPER SCARY ART

These scary projects will get you into art big time! You don't have to be great at drawing either— just follow these easy steps. Have fun, then step back and admire your creations!

TOP TIPS

1 Prepare different sizes of newspaper or paper towel strips before you get sticky hands.

2 Protect surfaces from dripping paint and glue. A plastic tablecoth is great, but an old towel or cardboard works well too.

3 Clean brushes in three small jars of water before using a different color of paint. Clean most of the paint off in the first jar, finish cleaning in the second jar, and store in the third jar.

4 Cover your models with a final layer of PVA glue. This will dry clear and protect the surface of your creation.

5 Use scraps of cardboard to mix your paint and save time washing up!

MATERIALS

In most of these projects you will need the papier-mâché glue and either newspaper strips of various sizes or strips of absorbent paper towel. Before starting, spend a little time preparing the paper strips so they're ready to use.

Masking tape Use it to shape and attach different parts of the model together. Two rolls will be enough to do most of the projects in this book.

PVA glue It's water-based, so it's easy to clean up.

Pipe cleaners Use 12 inch (30 cm) pipe cleaners.

Elastic bands and binder clips Useful for holding things in place while gluing and shaping.

Paper towel or facial tissue Use for a smooth final mâché layer and for stuffing, lining, and shaping models.

Newspaper Use for strong layers of mâché and construction.

Cardboard paper towel roll Use for construction and making small body parts.

Cardboard Cereal boxes and wavy packing cardboard are easy to cut.

Paper clips or thin wire Use to make small accessories.

Beads Use for eyes if you need them.

String Use for decoration and construction.

Craft sticks (optional)

Large stone or pebble

Small jar or yogurt container

Vegetable bag (netted)

Black plastic bag

METHOD

Tip: Work in one small area at a time.

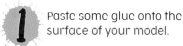 Paste some glue onto the surface of your model.

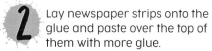 Lay newspaper strips onto the glue and paste over the top of them with more glue.

3 Cover with two layers of paper and allow to dry.

4 Add a final layer of papier-mâché and then cover with strips of paper towel for a smoother finish. Leave to dry before painting.

Note: Smaller projects will only need one layer of mâché.

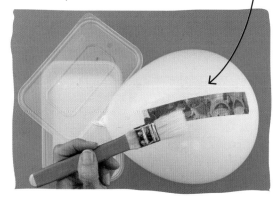

A GOOD RECIPE FOR PAPIER-MÂCHÉ GLUE

This quantity will be enough to complete a number of projects, but you may have to mix the recipe twice for the larger projects. Keep leftover glue in an airtight plastic container and store in a cool place. Stir well before using again.

1 cup (237 ml) of flour
1 1/2 cups (355 ml) of water
1/2 tablespoon (7 ml) of salt (add in humid climates to prevent mold)
1 cup (237 ml) of PVA glue
1 tablesoon (15 ml) of corn flour

1 Measure out the above ingredients into a plastic bowl or container.
2 Mix together well and store in an airtight container.

ADDITIONAL MATERIALS

Papier-mâché powder You can buy this very fine powder at most craft stores and online. You just mix with water and leave for an hour before using. Use mainly for fine detail and small projects. When it air-dries, it's ready for painting.

Paper clay (optional) This is a great alternative to the papier-mâché powder and is excellent for smaller projects and fine detail. Making it is quite messy and time consuming, so it is best to buy this from a craft store. A little goes a long way!

GARGOYLE DOOR DECORATION

This super scary door decoration is a great way to keep trespassers out of your room!

MATERIALS

Cereal box (enough cardboard to make two Gargoyle faces)

Craft sticks (optional—you can use plain cardstock)

1 sheet of paper

Thick cardboard

Papier-mâché glue and paper towel (see page 7)

Facial tissue or papier-mâché powder

PVA Glue

Paint

String or ribbon

Masking tape

1 Make a paper template for the gargoyle.

2 Draw around the paper template onto your cardboard twice. Cut out two faces, and cut out a rectangular message board.

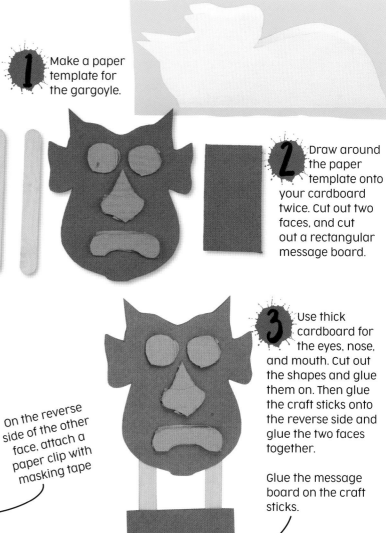

3 Use thick cardboard for the eyes, nose, and mouth. Cut out the shapes and glue them on. Then glue the craft sticks onto the reverse side and glue the two faces together.

Glue the message board on the craft sticks.

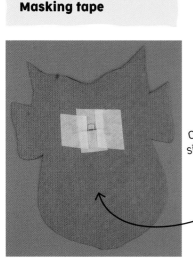

On the reverse side of the other face, attach a paper clip with masking tape

4 Cover the face and message board in two layers of mâché, avoiding the paper clip. Build up the facial features using facial tissue soaked in mâché glue or use papier-mâché powder (see page 7). Let dry before painting.

5 Paint your scary gargoyle and leave it to dry. Then thread the string through the paperclip, write a "Keep Out, Gargoyles Only" message, and hang it on your bedroom door!

KEEP OUT GARGOYLES ONLY

SCARY SPIDER FAMILY PAPERWEIGHT

MATERIALS

Large stone
Pipe cleaners
Paper clay (see page 7)
Fine-tip pen
PVA glue
Paper

Do the papers on your desk keep falling on the floor or blowing away? This scary spider paperweight is a great way to keep your papers in one place.

1 Practice drawing a web on paper first, then try drawing it onto the stone in pencil.

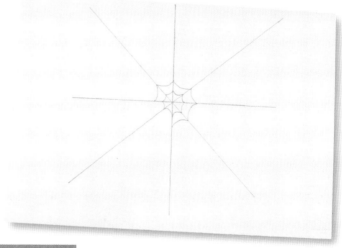

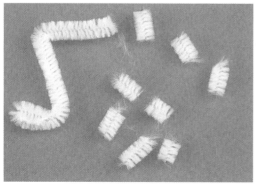

2 Use pipe cleaners to make eight legs and then cut another two pipe cleaners into small pieces.

3 Use paper clay to make the oval body of your spiders, one large and one small.

Carve out a mouth and eyes.

4 Push the eight legs into the clay of the larger spider and the small pieces onto the back of both spiders. Allow them to harden before painting.

5 Paint your stone white. When dry, draw the spider web at one end.

6 Paint a black semicircle for the spiders' cave and let it dry. Dip a sponge into a light sandy color paint, then press it onto paper towel to take off most of the paint. Sponge on a triangular shape. Highlight the tip of the triangle in the same way with white paint, and then paint a little spider.

Position the baby spider on the other end and draw his legs onto the stone

7 Paint your spiders and glue them onto the stone!

Tip: practice drawing your web on rough paper first for a perfect finish

UGLY FISH BANK

This very ugly fish is easy to make and it's the perfect place to keep your hard-earned money. It is surprising how quickly you can save money when you use an ugly fish bank!

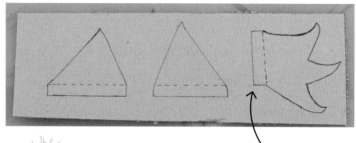

MATERIALS

Cardboard

Balloon

Cap with a rim (this came from a baking soda product)

Marker or felt-tip pen

Papier-mâché glue and newspaper strips (enough for two mâché layers)

Paper towel

Cardboard

Facial tissue or papier-mâché powder mix

1 On stiff cardboard draw the shapes above. Then cut out the shapes and fold along the dotted lines.

Tape the folded edge onto the balloon

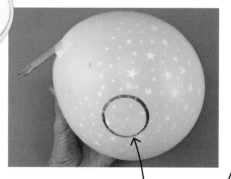

Tape on the fins with masking tape.

2 Inflate a balloon and attach the tail at the tied end with masking tape. Then cover the tie with more tape.

At the bottom of the balloon draw around the cap as shown, and just above the tail draw the shape of the coin slot.

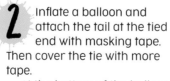

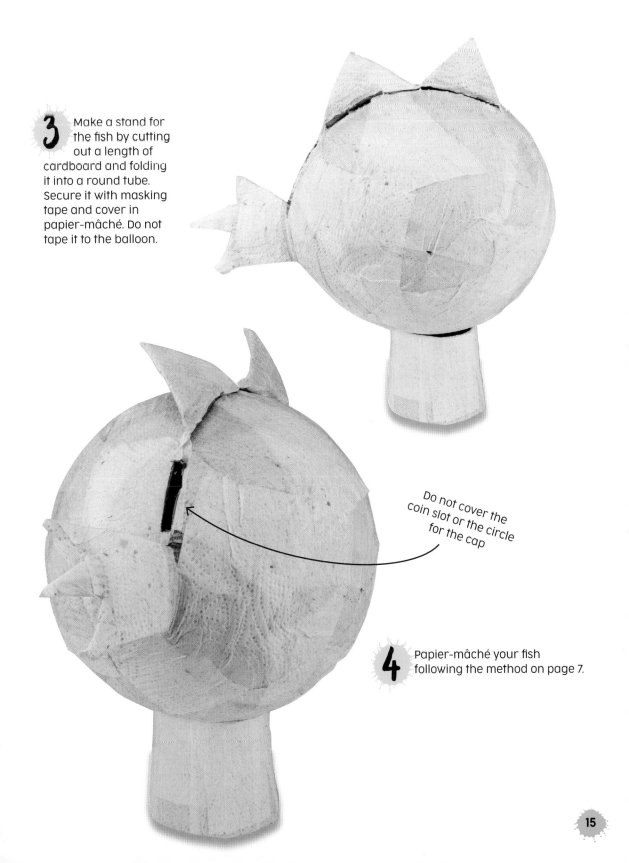

3 Make a stand for the fish by cutting out a length of cardboard and folding it into a round tube. Secure it with masking tape and cover in papier-mâché. Do not tape it to the balloon.

Do not cover the coin slot or the circle for the cap

4 Papier-mâché your fish following the method on page 7.

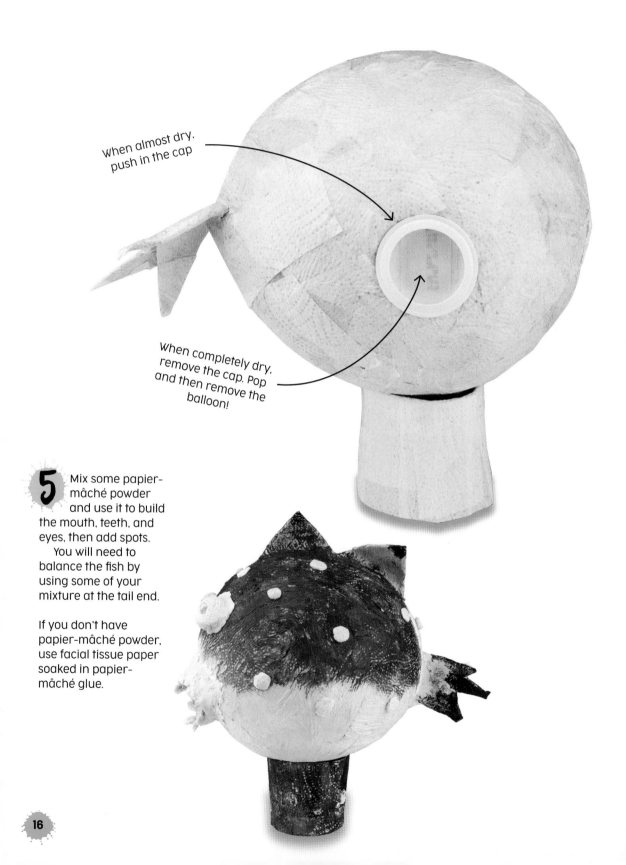

When almost dry, push in the cap

When completely dry, remove the cap. Pop and then remove the balloon!

5 Mix some papier-mâché powder and use it to build the mouth, teeth, and eyes, then add spots. You will need to balance the fish by using some of your mixture at the tail end.

If you don't have papier-mâché powder, use facial tissue paper soaked in papier-mâché glue.

Go wild painting your fish and get ready to start saving! You can retrieve your money easily by removing the cap.

Be a champion ugly fish saver!

All donations welcome!

FRANKENSTEIN COAT HANGER

Meet Frank! Imagine the surprise anyone will have opening your closet and finding Frankenstein hanging from the rack, looking after your clothes!

MATERIALS

Coat hanger
Paper
Cardboard
Papier-mâché glue and paper towel
Mâché powder mix or facial tissue soaked in glue
Strong tape
Pipe cleaners
String
Fine-tip pen

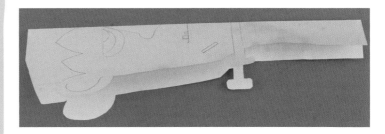

1 Draw and cut out a Frankenstein-shaped template on paper.

2 Draw around your template onto cardboard. Use a fine-tip pen to draw the hairline and features. Cover both sides in a thin layer of papier-mâché, using paper towel, and leave to dry.

You can see Frank's details through the mâché layer. Mix your papier-mâché powder and use it to construct the eyes, nose, scars, teeth, and bolts.

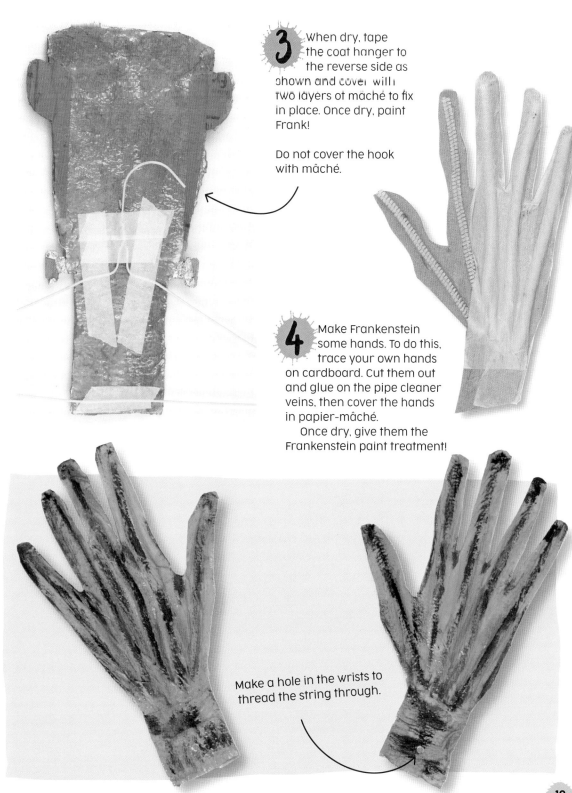

3 When dry, tape the coat hanger to the reverse side as shown and cover with two layers of mâché to fix in place. Once dry, paint Frank!

Do not cover the hook with mâché.

4 Make Frankenstein some hands. To do this, trace your own hands on cardboard. Cut them out and glue on the pipe cleaner veins, then cover the hands in papier-mâché.
   Once dry, give them the Frankenstein paint treatment!

Make a hole in the wrists to thread the string through.

FRANKENSTEIN COAT HANGER

To make this a great scary coat hanger, you need to complete him by joining his hands and head together as shown below.

Shade areas using a sponge. Dab the sponge on paper towel first to take off most of the paint

5 First tie some string to each side of the hanger—make sure the string is longer than the sleeves. Then place the head and coat hanger in your garment. Thread the string down through the sleeves.

Then thread the string through the holes in the hands, making sure they are the correct length for the hands to show at the end of the sleeves.

He is now ready to hang out in your room!

Give him a final coat of PVA glue to make him good and strong

BASKET SKULL

Here is a great desk game to play at Halloween or any time of the year. The skeleton's skull is the basketball!

MATERIALS

For the skeleton:
Stiff cardboard
Pipe cleaners
Masking tape
Paint
Cotton ball or balled-up facial tissue
String

For the basketball net:
Pipe cleaner
Vegetable bag (netted)
Long cardboard tube from plastic wrap or tin foil
Masking tape
Paint
String
Papier-mâché glue and paper towel

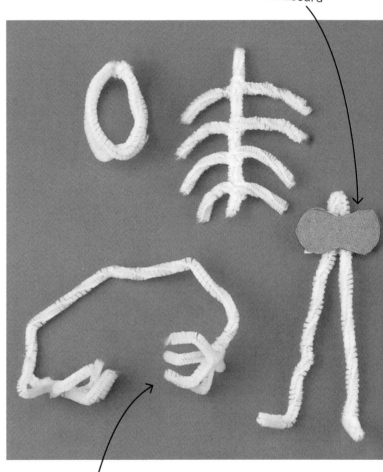

Cut out the hips from cardboard

Make the body parts as shown (the head is two loops, one over the other)

1 To strengthen your skeleton you need to double up your pipe cleaners by winding one around another.

Use one for the legs, one for the arms, one or two for the ribs, one for the head, and the last one for the hands

2 Stuff the skull with a cotton ball or balled up facial tissue and add string for the hair.
Carefully wrap the skull in masking tape (cut the tape in half and use smaller strips).

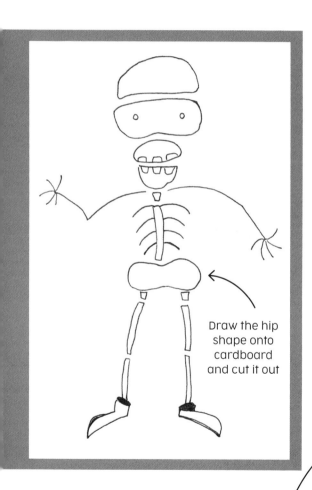

Draw the hip shape onto cardboard and cut it out

Make a base out of stiff cardboard. Glue the tube to the base

3 Tape the hips onto the legs with masking tape.
Attach the bottom of the ribs to the legs with masking tape.
Wind the arms around the top of the ribs.

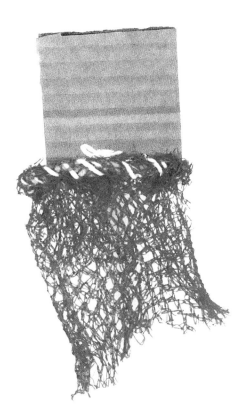

4 For the basketball net, make a backboard out of stiff cardboard. Measure and make two slits in the backboard so you can slide it onto the tube.

Make a basketball hoop with a pipe cleaner and attach to the tube with masking tape.

Add the netting to the hoop and attach by winding the string in and out of the hoop and net.

Cover the base with papier-mâché for added strength before painting

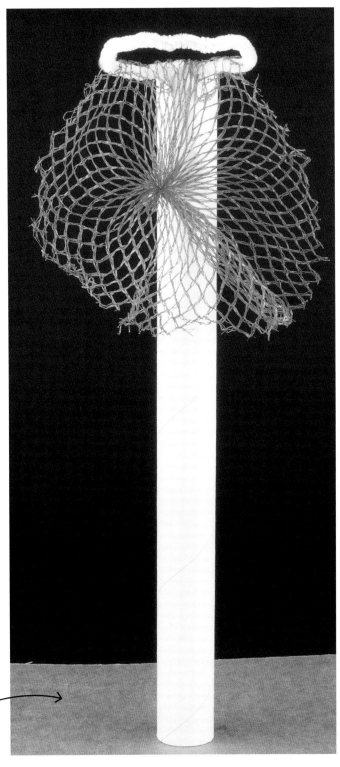

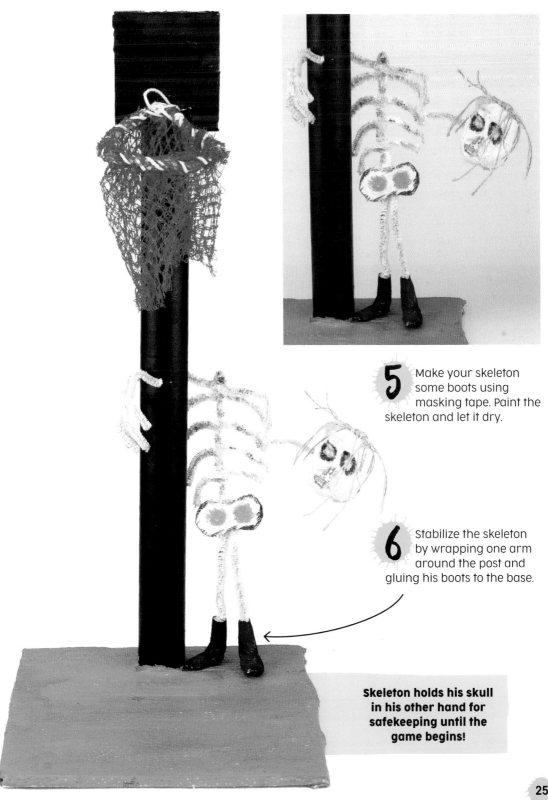

5 Make your skeleton some boots using masking tape. Paint the skeleton and let it dry.

6 Stabilize the skeleton by wrapping one arm around the post and gluing his boots to the base.

Skeleton holds his skull in his other hand for safekeeping until the game begins!

MONSTER PEN PAL

This is one of the easiest items to make in the book. Just five simple steps make a monster pen pal to keep your pens stored in a handy place!

1 On the cardboard, draw around the base of your jar, then draw some monster toes. Cut out the shape.

2 Start to mold the clay around your pot, covering up to the rim.
    Paper clay is easy to carve and shape.

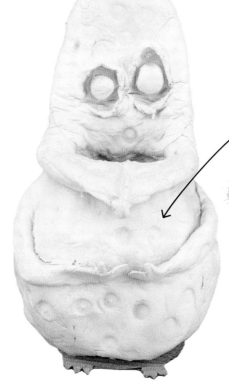

Give your pen pal some spotty dents all over with the end of a pencil

3 Make some arms and little hands and press them onto the body.
    Build up the rim of your pot to make great big lips, and build up the head with more clay.

Put some clay toes on the base

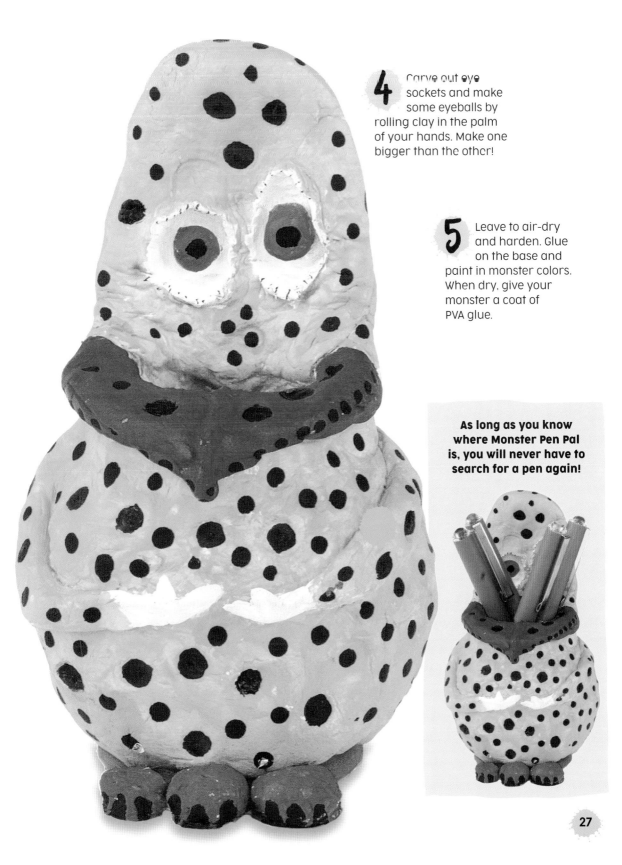

4 Carve out eye sockets and make some eyeballs by rolling clay in the palm of your hands. Make one bigger than the other!

5 Leave to air-dry and harden. Glue on the base and paint in monster colors. When dry, give your monster a coat of PVA glue.

As long as you know where Monster Pen Pal is, you will never have to search for a pen again!

BEASTLY BATS

Some blood-sucking bats are always a favorite around the house. These two will make great pets—or you can make more to create your own bat colony.

MATERIALS

Stiff cardboard

Cardboard toilet paper rolls

Cotton ball or facial tissue

Pipe cleaners

Black plastic garbage bag

Masking tape

PVA glue

Beads

Paper

Papier-mâché glue and paper towel

String or wire

Paint

FLYING BAT

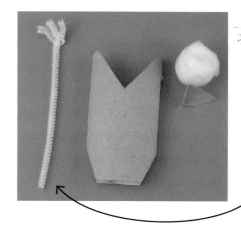

1 Flatten the cardboard toilet paper roll, draw on this shape, and cut out the body as shown. Cut out some ears from the scraps.

Make two legs and feet out of pipe cleaners

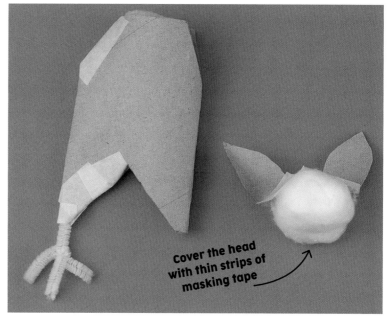

2 Use masking tape to attach the legs inside the body and attach the ears to the cotton ball head. Stuff the body with cotton balls or facial tissue and seal the ends with masking tape.

Cover the head with thin strips of masking tape

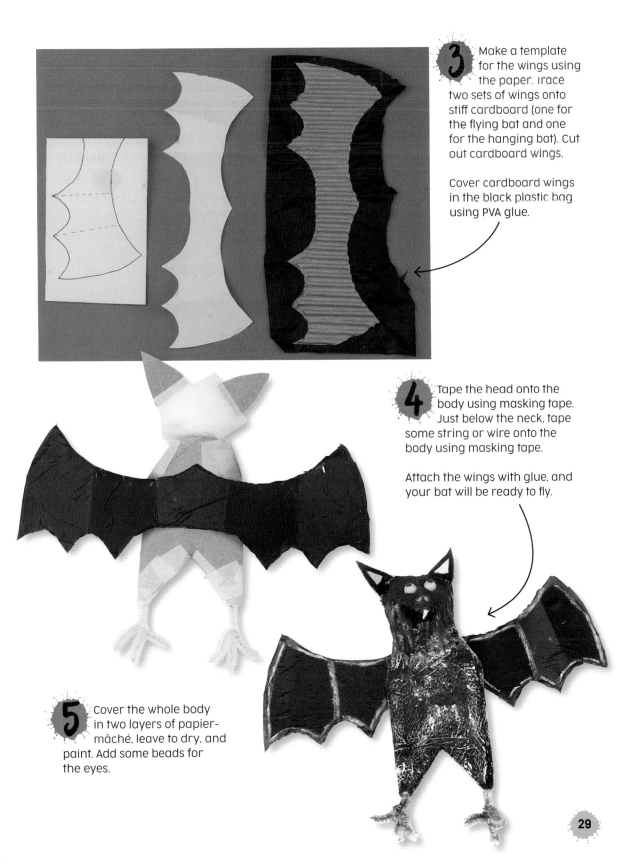

3 Make a template for the wings using the paper. Trace two sets of wings onto stiff cardboard (one for the flying bat and one for the hanging bat). Cut out cardboard wings.

Cover cardboard wings in the black plastic bag using PVA glue.

4 Tape the head onto the body using masking tape. Just below the neck, tape some string or wire onto the body using masking tape.

Attach the wings with glue, and your bat will be ready to fly.

5 Cover the whole body in two layers of papier-mâché, leave to dry, and paint. Add some beads for the eyes.

HANGING BAT

6 Flatten the cardboard toilet paper roll, but this time draw a line as shown. Then cut along the line to make a thinner body.

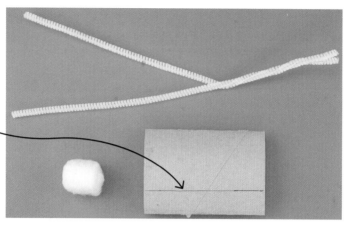

Cover with papier-mâché and let it dry

8 Stuff the body with cotton balls or facial tissue as before. Make a head, cover in masking tape, and attach to the body.

7 Cut out the shape as shown and make some legs and feet. Attach them inside the body with masking tape. Tape and seal the open edge to the side and at the feet end.

9 Paint your hanging bat, add beads for the eyes, glue on the wings, and fold them as shown.

Make a cool colony
of bats to hang out
with you!

SUPPLIES

BRUSHES

1 brush specifically to use for glue
1 fine paintbrush for detail
2 medium paintbrushes
1 large paintbrush Use an old decorating paintbrush to mâché the larger projects.

PAINT

Acrylic paints (used for most of the projects)
Watercolor paints

USEFUL ITEMS

3 water jars for cleaning brushes
1 water jar for the glue brush
Plastic airtight container to store glue (small ice cream container or similar)
Mixing bowl for mâché (any medium plastic container)
2 Measuring cups for mâché mix (paper cups, one for the dry ingredient and one for the glue)
Pencils
Fine-tip pen
Sponge brush
Ruler
Scissors
Plain tape
Felt-tip or acrylic pens

THE AUTHOR

Emily Kington has worked in publishing and children's books for over twenty years. She loves art and is passionate about making art accessible for children and engaging them in a variety of different art forms. Emily lives in England with her husband and two children and loves outdoor sports, traveling, and good food.